COACHING POETRY
FROM A SPIRITUAL PATH

John
Blakey

Coaching Poetry from a Spiritual Path

By John Blakey

ISBN: 978-1-291-35533-8

Copyright © 2013 John Blakey

All rights reserved. No part of this publication may be reproduced, stored in a retrieval system, or transmitted, in any form or by any means, electronic, mechanical, photocopying, recording and/or otherwise without prior written permission of the author. This book may not be lent, resold, hired out or otherwise disposed of by way of trade in any form, binding or cover other than that in which it is published, without the prior consent of the author.

*To God Only
the Glory*

Contents

Preface i

Bring it Home 1

Closer 3

Biting the Strawberry 5

Birds on the Runway 7

The Hinterland 9

River Deep, Mountain High 11

Confessions of the Western Psyche 13

Maybe it's Going to be Alright? 15

New Born 17

Defenceless and Waiting 19

Keep Me Sane 21

Warm Tears 23

High and Mighty 25

Leap before you Look 27

Remorseless Joy 29

Books 31

A Thousand Names for Joy 33

Partnerships 35

Beyond the Bridge 37

The Long Goodbye 39

The Return Path 41

Learning to Love Failure 43

Forever Ours to Keep 45

F.A.T.E. - From All Thoughts Everywhere	47
Transition Throes	49
Methodical Recklessness	51
Reclamation	53
Glittering Prize	55
The Word	57
The Morally Brave	59
Sleep, Dream, Wake, Sleep, Dream	61
Redemption Song	63
All	65
Soulburst	67
Barbaric Garb	69
The Narrow Gate	71
Letting You Down	73
Fight, Flight or Forgiveness	75
A Labour of Love	77
A Stumbling Grace	79
Ha Ha English	81
Friend or Foe	83
The Gold	85
Against the Grain	87
Freedom to Live	89
Cloying Vines	91
The Dogs are Coming	93
Lamentation	95
Facing it Down	97
Letting Go	99

From Sense to Nonsense ....….…. 101
Dissociation 103
The Watchmen and the Wolves 105
About the Author 108

Preface

For many years I have been a private poet and a private Christian. When it came to sharing either my poetry or my Christianity my lips would be mysteriously sealed and fear would strike my heart. The fear of judgement and ridicule: 'Who are you to be a poet? Who are you to believe in Jesus Christ?'

Slowly, I have tip-toed to the edge. I have gradually built the confidence to share my writing more widely and I have realised that, whilst not everyone is a Christian and not everyone appreciates my poetry, some people are and some people do. With the publishing of this book I have finally 'come out' and jumped off the edge of my private cliff. In so doing, I hope that the words of the American writer Ray Bradbury prove to be true: 'You've got to jump off cliffs all the time and build your wings on the way down.'

The poems themselves were written over a period of many years and the commentaries were added when I started featuring them on my blog in the period 2009-2011. Since I am an executive coach, many of the poems are focused on the themes of personal development, transformation and the challenges involved in achieving courageous goals. You do not need to be a Christian in order to appreciate these words, but there are occasional references to scripture and Christian concepts, which reveal my original inspiration.

Finally, from scripture I take inspiration from these words from the book of Isaiah: 'Then one of the seraphs flew to me with a live coal in his hand...With it he touched my mouth and said 'See, this has touched your lips; your guilt is taken away and your sin atoned for'. Then I heard the voice of the Lord saying 'Whom shall I send? And who will go for us?' And I said 'Here am I. Send me!' (Isaiah 6: 6-8). Wherever you are on your own spiritual path, I wish you god speed with your own next step.

Bring it Home

BRING IT HOME,
That which we have found,
Bring it home,
Make the stories shorter,
For you are the seed,
And this is your garden, your backyard,
Let them know that the knot has torn open,
That which bound our vision,
Let them know that the gates have swung free,
There is no other side of life,
There is no dark side of the moon,
Save in our child-like dreams.
Bring it home,
Make the stories shorter,
For here is the heart of our concerns,
The cradle of our courage,
Amongst the love that has not been forgotten,
And the lives not left behind.

This poem is difficult to grasp at first read. It comes from the depths! It is open to many interpretations, one of which is that it is speaking of the end of a heroic journey when the hero must return home, and home is where the heart is. The 'stories' referred to are the dramas and adventures of everyday life. 'Make the stories shorter' refers to e s c a p i n g the drama and returning to the things and the people who are really important. These people are often close by, but are ignored or neglected in the rush to make an impression in the world. The hero also returns with good news from his/her travels, 'the knot has torn open', the dramas we were taught as children are not necessarily true; they are modern myths that keep us small. And the alternative to coming home is to leave others behind and to forget the love. How many of us have done this then realised our mistake too late?

Closer

SO FAR NOW, SO far now,
From the tents below,
Beyond the tiny point,
Of no return,
A bridge collapses behind,
A rock falls past in silence,
To leave the sound of breathing,
Breathing in, breathing out,
Where are we taking we?
With our new lungs and limbs,
Where are we taking we?
In this matrix of opportunity,
What keeps us going?
Save the spiritual rope between us,
What keeps us going?
Save the thrill of tomorrow,
And looking out on a new sky,
And pausing to drink in our laughter and say our prayers,
Before committing ourselves again,
To find our highest selves in this changing world.

This poem uses the metaphor of mountaineering to explore a journey of personal development. The 'tents below' represent the starting point of the journey, and the 'collapsing bridge' means that there is now no way back. The traveller is left transfixed, frightened, yet exhilarated, by the possibility of going further. The poem shifts from the 'I' to the 'we' as the traveller recognises that he/she is not alone. There are other travellers on the mountainside, and in that realisation can be found strength, excitement and laughter, as well as the shared will to move forward another step.

Biting the Strawberry

IF I SNAPPED OFF the future claims,
And the past travails from this holy instant of now,
I can sort of see how something new would break free,
Something fearless, smiling and aglow,
If I could live in that space in between,
Then I can sort of see,
How my bruises would be healed,
And my expectations rendered obsolete,
Yes, I can sort of grope for this new domain,
And I can sort of open the door,
Sort of free and straight and star-spangled light,
Sort of born again in each moment's grace,
Sort of heaven, sort of nice.

The title of this poem comes from this zen koan:- 'A man travelling across a field encountered a tiger. He fled and the tiger fled after him. Coming to a precipice, he caught hold of the root of a wild vine and swung himself down over the edge. The tiger sniffed at him from above. Trembling, the man looked down to where, far below, another tiger was waiting to eat him. Only the vine sustained him. Two mice, one white and one black, little by little started to gnaw away the vine. The man saw a luscious strawberry near him. Grasping the vine with one hand, he plucked the strawberry with the other. How sweet it tasted!' It is about living in the present moment; the 'space in between' is the present moment, which lies between past bruises and future expectations. The repetitive use of the phrase 'sort of' implies that, on the one hand, this feels like an easy step to make but, on the other, it is strange and full of trepidation. The fear of who we really are?

Birds on the Runway

A THIN VEIL, a cloudy sky,
The flutter of settling wings,
Birds that stall our progress,
Like mice and lice and other little things,
Strange mix of phobia and respect,
Welds us to a past we loathe,
And yet they wait for us,
Those smiling faces on the other side,
Forever waiting, forever smiling,
Forever hoping and keeping faith,
Sketching the good times to come,
How could we let them down?
How could we mothball our dusty engines?
We scatterers of the birds,
We clearers of the mist,
When will we change our minds,

And honour our forgotten selves?
When will we stop using our past learning,
As the light to guide us now?

The inspiration for this poem came from looking out of the window of an aeroplane as it taxied down the runway, and seeing a huge flock of birds suddenly take off from the concrete as the plane revved up its engines. It is a metaphor for all the little things that can get in the way of us fulfilling our potential - so many excuses for not unleashing our true selves. Why do we do this? Because we are 'welded to a past we loathe'. Yet we know there are people who have fulfilled their potential, we know how happy it has made them and we know they believe we could do the same. The poem challenges the reader to start to move forward, to clear the mist, to scatter the birds. The last two lines are taken from the book 'A Course in Miracles', and they challenge the limiting belief that past experience is the best guide to future possibilities.

The Hinterland

TO NOT INVADE NOR be invaded,
To realise what I am does not need defending,
For it is eternal and invulnerable,
To stand on the border of you and I,
And stand down all the armies that led me here,
Firm and upright and looking you in the eye,
To feel the power that flows through me,
Yet to know that it will not consume me,
Nor will I be tempted to use it irresponsibly,
Nor will I shy away from it such that others will lay false claim,
And there to balance the polarities in me,
Recognise, be with and then unite,
A masculine feminine red blue left right hot cold composite,
And here to live and breathe,
Connected to my source in joy and release,
Not fixing you nor being fixed,
Not caring nor caring not,
Not rushing on nor rushing back,
Not looking away nor staring down,
Blazing in a neutral glory as God intended me to be,
Like a flower opening its petals to the sun,
Giving without ego, receiving without guilt,
Breathing in and breathing out,
Like a tide that ebbs and flows around its core,
And knowing that in this space all who find me will find themselves,
All who reach out will be reaching in,
All that could be will forever be,
As gently in forgiveness a healing stream washes through this world,
When we stand together in the hinterland.

This poem uses the metaphor of the hinterland - the undeveloped, rural land outlying a coastal port. What might we find in the hinterland of personal relationships? Relationships that are based on mutual respect and diversity, rather than the need to dominate others or be dominated by them. Many relationships are grounded in fear. To deal with the fear, a person chooses to attack another or to get their defence in first. It is a cycle that we all have learnt as a way of getting by, but ultimately it leads to war between people, between groups, between organisations and between nations. Some give away their power too easily for fear of its potential. Some steal the power of others for fear that they don't have enough for themselves. The poem challenges this world view and challenges the reader to find the power within, to claim this honestly, but to use it responsibly. This then is a natural, sustainable power and beauty; like that of a flower, like that of the tide. It is a hugely attractive power because of the example it sets to others. It leads to reconciliation, forgiveness and intimacy.

River Deep, Mountain High

BE AT YOUR MOUNTAIN top,
Let the plains be flooded with your bless-ed energy,
Let the clouds take your heavenly shape,
Be at your mountain top,
In the fullness of your creation,
In the bloom of your latency,
Be at your mountain top,
And I will be at mine,
And as you survey this wondrous scene,
Our eyes will meet and greet within,
The waters will surge in the valley of our dreams,
And we will lift our world unto a new domain,
Forever each one of us.

Like the poem 'Closer', these words use the mountains, clouds and landscapes to create a metaphor for self-actualisation at both the individual and collective level. The 'wondrous scene' is the prospect of so many million mountain tops stretching into the distance, so many million self-actualised individuals, each with their unique beauty and full self-expression. At the point of mutual recognition, the 'meeting of the eyes', a deep stirring in the collective unconscious is triggered. The metaphor of a rising, flooding energy hints at a shift in consciousness, a new world, a new domain. There is a feeling of pure joy at this prospect.

Confessions of the Western Psyche

WISH I WAS BORN a black man,
Without the guilt of bleaching skin,
Wish I was born a Muslim,
Without the shame of Christian hands,
Wish I was born a woman,
Without the hard-wired, violent head,
Wish I wasn't this demagogue, this hulking ego-beast,
Wish I wasn't a slave-master, an empire-building thief,
Wish I hadn't dropped the A-bomb,
On all those yellow-skinned folk,
Wish I wasn't so clever,
So full of tricks and lies,
Wish I wasn't so far West,
That I am scared to kneel and pray,
But more, much more, than this,
I just wish two thirds of the world could forgive me,
For 2,000 years of pain.

This is an angry poem written from the perspective of the white Anglo-Saxon protestant (WASP) male; that collective identity that has placed itself as the 'top dog' in the world and ensured that there are plenty of 'bottom dogs' on which to prey, whether that be on the grounds of gender, race or religion. And, of course, I am a WASP myself, so this is within me to some degree, it is in my genes and my conditioning. I know how it is possible to use the intellect as a means to post-rationalise loveless acts because I have done it myself and continue to do so to various degrees. For 30 years I too was too scared to 'kneel and pray', i.e. to admit the possibility that there might be something more powerful in the universe than the human will and the human brain. If I can feel this anger in me at some level when I am one of the 'top dogs' myself, then maybe it gives me a glimpse into how it feels to have been on the other side of the cultural divide for 2,000 years. What anger lurks in those hidden depths?

Maybe it's Going to be Alright?

WHAT IF IT WERE going to be alright?
At the end of the day,
What if you could not fail?
To live your life,
To be yourself,
What if it will all be taken care of?

With or without you,
One way or another,
What if it isn't your job?
To save the world,
To make me happy,
What if it really doesn't matter?

What you achieve,
What you obtain,
Who the hell you think you are?

In these imagined spaces of the psyche,
The gaps between synapses yet to form,
Lies a strange, unchartered path,
A path which draws me into its mystery,
Charms me with its innocence,
What if I were to venture down its course?
In the glow of personal freedom,
With the lightness of a baby step,
What if the peace that laps at the edge of nothingness,
Was a permanent ocean of joy magnificent?

This poem was written whilst waiting for a flight in Heathrow's terminal 5 - a great space for writing! It is about faith and humility. The faith to trust that we don't need to strive fearfully, that other people are on their chosen path and that the world will keep spinning regardless of the human will. The faith to believe that, despite our worries, it is possible that we will die with a smile on our faces. The humility to recognise that our story, however dramatic, will be washed away in the blink of an eye. These ideas scare the ego silly and challenge existing belief systems. The 'gaps between the synapses' refers to the scope for new belief systems to be created in our minds, new beliefs that reflect these ideas. New links between neural synapses, new ways of thinking, new 'paths'. Creation. The 'nothingness' referred to in the last lines refers to the death of the ego. The 'joy magnificent' is the peace of God, if that is a language that appeals to you.

New Born

THESE STORIES CAN BE revealed,
Now that peace has broken the seal,
Our ancestors' fighting and our mothers' screaming,
Are long ago in our consciousness,
We are rising like a cork escaping a wreck,
We are rising like a heaving chest,
We lay our shock at the door of the truth,
And know what we knew not,
Letting it pass like clouds and thunder rain.
A torrent of violent emotion spills us past,
Yet we are not drowning any more,
What once overwhelmed is now knee deep,
Retains no power, no vengeance, no recurrent tide,
What once hypnotised our vulnerable minds,
Now spins child-like to the floor,
A tantrum of a willful, unbridled nano-sense,
A belch in an eternity of grace,
A hiccup, a distortion, a perturbing crease,
Amidst the still, crisp perfection of cradling hands,
And so we lightly close the door,
On a child's last feint sobs and red stained eyes,
Inviting sleep to erase the day's devils, its dogma, its dramatic turns,
Trusting in the clean slate of tomorrow,
And in our forgetful, forgiving selves.
Trusting in the benign universal space,
And the first smile of a new-born face.

Well, what can I say about this poem? Like many of my poems, these words are about the possibility of transformation, of escaping from the past with all its frightening memories. Not only at an individual level, but also at a collective level. The poem describes a feeling of having emerged from a traumatic history to gain a new perspective and then leaving this history behind, once and for all. The trigger for this possibility is a period of peace ('Now that peace has broken the seal'), the likes of which we have been fortunate to experience in our lifetimes in the Western world. A history which once overwhelmed us and controlled us, and was therefore acted out over and over again, is no longer in the driving seat. This history is likened to a child-like state of mind, a temporary stage from which we can grow up. It is also positioned as a peculiarly human stage that we have created amongst a wider universe that does not share our tantrums, but instead looks on and waits for them to pass, waits for normal service to be resumed ('amidst the still, crisp perfection of cradling hands'). The poem closes with the image of a parent leaving an upset child just before they fall asleep. As every parent knows, the child wakes up in the morning having forgotten and forgiven, having wiped the slate clean - fresh, hopeful and smiling! A wonderful vision for the human race.

Defenceless and Waiting

I OPEN MY arms,
And drop all defences,
Weapons that clatter to the floor,
But you keep coming at me,
To leave feints and whirls, ducks and dives,
We can play this game all day,
If you really want to,
If you really want to,
All those hours of sweaty practice,
Through raining blows,
Now you see me, now you don't,
We can play this game all day,
If you really want to,
If you really want to,
Yet outside the sun is shining,
The birds are singing,
God is creating in all his glory,
Children are crying for a better world,
Yelling for us to stop it,
Stop it now you foolish fighting men,
If you really want to,
If you really want to,
For a pregnant future awaits your choice,
If you really want it,
If you really want it.

This poem was written following a conversation with a friend who is focusing her coaching work on 'helping high achievers deliver results without creating collateral damage'. Our conversation reminded me of this poem, which is a metaphor for working with 'alpha mammalians'. Such leaders are often male, but not exclusively so. This type of leader tends to want to fight with you, if not physically then mentally. Everything is a competition and everything leads to either domination or being dominated, to win or lose, to victory or defeat. This is the only lens through which they appear to view the world. With many years of t'ai chi training, I am familiar with t'ai chi as a self-defence technique. The poem visualises my employment of such techniques to avoid being defeated, but growing so tired of this game that I am at the point of giving up ('I open my palms, And drop all defences, Weapons that clatter to the floor'). Beyond this point, you simply use feints, side-steps and sleight of hand to avoid being hurt; again, this should be interpreted at the emotional and soulful level, although it is presented in physical language. Meanwhile, outside of this energetic cameo, the world is in a mess and there are many, many problems that must be solved through reaching beyond the 'win/lose' paradigm. A different future is possible, but the poem questions the will of the alpha mammalian ('If you really want it'). Does the alpha mammalian simply enjoy fighting too much to give it up on behalf of a more sustainable future? We shall see.

Keep Me Sane

MEMORIES OF A FIGHTING world,
Litter the hall,
The spikes and sharp objects of another life,
When wedded to my status and my achievements,
I forgot how to breathe, how to care, how to love,
……..and be loved,
……..and be cared for.

One night woke with my own hand grasping my throat,
One night woke driving a hot poker through my own heart,
Life fighting life fighting life,
Trying to prove a point that was already proven,
Like a mad dog chasing its tail,
And not sensing the whole that is self-evident
……..evident self,
……..evident life.

Pray keep me sane,
Far from the maddening crowd,
Pray keep me feeling this breath,
And tending to the little things,
Whilst giving my all to the All,
Pray keep me sane,
Amidst all these fantastic illusions,
For I know that from this vantage point,
I can share in the grander will and be the innocent blossoming of life,
I was born to be,
……born to be,
……born to BE!

This is passionate poem, a passionate plea. Having glimpsed release from worldly temptations (status, achievements, etc.), there is always the risk of falling back and becoming insanely attached to them again; attached to the outcomes, attached to the pain of a competitive, fragmented life. The poem highlights the self-defeating nature of such a vicious circle, the absurd use of consciousness to create an 'unwinnable' illusion versus an alternative perspective where the focus is on the little things, like care and love and breath and giving, and a letting go to that which is greater than you, whatever you might call that. The final line reminds me of the phrase that we are first and foremost human beings not human 'doings'. It is in the 'being' not the 'doing' that we can stay sane.

Warm Tears

FALLING LIKE WARM tears,
Your words bless the ground we're stood upon,
Like a warm hand grasped,
You sense the life and truth within,
And all recedes, contracts, withdraws,
Against this endearing declaration,
All egos cower and hunker down,
Like so many warm tears falling,
On the fires of this earth.

Pick up this torch my friend,
For the next leg of the journey is yours,
And no one else has this route etched in their hearts,
Take courage from those who have gone before,
Take hope from those who will come,
On balance this was your choice,
And the many doors have closed behind,
On balance this was your calling,
And the many faces turn your way,
Like many warm tears falling,
Let your heart flood with joy,
Like many warm tears falling,
Drown out the craven world,
And as you step gingerly into your full, holy self,
Will we all bask in your radiance,
Will we all be halfway there.

This poem was written following a coffee in Starbucks with a fellow coach. We had one of those conversations that creates a connection, stirs your feelings and reminds you of a shared sense of purpose, but which also reminds you never to judge the path taken by another. Paths that might converge and diverge in a seemingly random fashion, yet reflect an individual choice, conscious or otherwise. As with many of my poems, the metaphor of water and floods and drowning is used to symbolise the rising spirit. In an interview shortly before his death, Jung said: 'What comes next? Aquarius, the Waterpourer, the falling of water from one place to another. And the little fish receiving the water from the pitcher of the Waterpourer....But there is danger in the water, on the banks'. Maybe the 'danger' that Jung was referring to was the risk of an over-reaction, an over-correction? Maybe it was something else? The poem closes with a hint that in finding our own individual fulfilment we inspire others to do the same, despite the apparent paradox of such a self-centred approach.

High and Mighty

FALLEN leaves,
Were they so proud?
In the height of summer,
Were they so green?
In their full bloom,
Now trodden underfoot,
Mulching and mushing away.

Tall trees,
Were they so humble?
In the height of summer,
Were they so browned-off?
Amidst their full blooming,
Now starkly defining the night sky,
Bold and brazen in their permanence.

This is a short poem about seasons and cycles - about how quickly the trappings of success, the 'leaves', can fall away. They have had their '15 minutes of fame', as the superficial foliage that comes and goes is admired then forgotten then trodden underfoot, whereas the tree that spawns the leaf is a different representation of success. Hidden for many months by the fluttering leaves, the tree's true beauty is only revealed in the winter when it stands proud and permanent, enduring the cycles, the seasons, and being the source, rather than the evidence, of growth. It prompts thoughts of what it means to be successful, how to react when you are praised or admired and how to sustain your beliefs when all seem to be against you.

Leap before you Look

THE STEPS THAT FREEZE us,
The illusion of barbed wire,
The sheer agony of becoming who we are,
Like a yawn, a stretch, a chasm,
You stare into the abyss of freedom,

And it stares into you,
Side by side,
With the birds on the runway,

Waiting for something to happen,
Forever watching a looping film,

Waiting for it to come to us,
We pray for the courage to take a tiny step,
We pray for the fresh air of liberation,
We pray for support and strength and grace,
As into an open future we fall.

I recently had the pleasure of attending a workshop with the corporate poet, David Whyte, who kept me spellbound for an entire day with his love of words, rhythm and intonation. One of the poems he recited to us, and my favourite of the day, was called 'Start Close In' (Start close in, Don't take the second step or the third, Start with the first thing, The step you don't want to take.'). 'Leap before you Look' has a similar message to 'Start Close In'. Both are poems about the first, terrifying step - the one you don't want to take - not the second or the third step, but the first step. They are both about finding your own path, not following someone else's heroics, creating your own destiny rather than 'waiting for something to happen', having the audaciousness to become that which only you are, not a pale imitation of someone else. A sister poem of 'Leap before you Look' is 'Birds on the Runway'. The 'birds' appear again in this poem as a metaphor for the little things that get in the way of the big things. The phrase 'you stare into the abyss of freedom and it stares into you' is a shameless copy of Nietzsche's comment '…if you gaze for long into an abyss, the abyss gazes also into you'.

Remorseless Joy

Slipping slowly and gracefully,
Long shadows and creeping time,
A cycle draws to a close,
A glorious, glorious time,
An era of great struggles, great achievement and great learning,

A long sunset to a shining day,
And tomorrow you wake up in a different world,
The new, the emerging, the implicate,
An open space, a blank sheet,
The looming gift to write new tunes,

As others gather in musty rooms,
Will you strike out with the edge of your creativity?
As others embrace familiarity,
Will you choose a strange, uncertain path?
And so the wheel turns and turns again.
Gathering pace then slowing down,
Propelled by the remorseless joy of our reinventing souls.

I recently read the book 'Nature and the Human Soul' by Bill Plotkin. It was an inspiring and challenging read, with many wonderful snippets of poetry scattered throughout the prose. Bill's premise is that life has many stages and that each stage feels like it is the best stage of life when you are in it. So much so, that individuals, groups and societies can cling to a stage far beyond its useful life. He suggests that Western society is trapped in a permanently adolescent stage with little access to the wisdom of later stages of life. This poem mirrors this feeling of transition from one day to another, from one stage of life to another. A great day draws to a close because this is the natural cycle and, in the morning, you start again with a blank sheet. And whilst there is an inevitable sadness associated with endings, there is always the excitement that follows with new beginnings, possibilities to create, to engage the unfamiliar. The last line of the poem highlights that sometimes, even though your mind and your heart might wish to stay in the known and the familiar, the soul can only find joy in the act of creation, and it is this that it seeks with patience, persistence and passion.

Books

THAT WHICH IS LEFT unexpressed,
Remains shrouded in doubt and question marks,
Let my faith not fall into this shadow land,
Let it be expressed with conviction, courage and clarity,
Without fear of critique or adulation,
So to align itself with the universal will,
That which brings forth the miraculous,
From the womb of a future, open and free.

Is that it? I had forgotten how short this poem was. Still, 'they don't make diamonds as big as bricks' as my mother used to say - God bless her soul. I have written books, on my own and with my colleague Ian Day, so this poem strikes a chord for me. Maybe it does for you too? The poem is about finding your voice and giving yourself the permission to express that which is in you to express, regardless of what other people might make of it. For anyone who has started a blog, written a book, composed a song, or simply presented to an audience that you respect, then the sentiment remains the same. Don't allow yourself to be placed in the 'shadow land' for fear that your truth will be criticised or that it will be praised. Some of us are frightened of failure, some of us are frightened of success, but as Kipling famously said: 'If you can meet with triumph and disaster, And treat those two impostors just the same…..you'll be a man, my son'. When you free yourself from these impostors then you are left simply with the joy of creation - that which brings forth the miraculous from the womb of a future, open and free.

A Thousand Names for Joy

WHAT IF THE WORLD was a reflection of my consciousness?
A mirror into which I peer and judge,
Each person a fragment of my own self,
Just an interpretation, a shadow, a vapour trail,
What if we were a temporary distortion of God's thoughtlessness?
Pieces in a puzzle we are creating,
Lovers in a game of our own making,
Just an expression of life's grand will,
From this mindset, where would we then explore?
Like animals again, dumb and free,
Living the living so painlessly,
Dying in the arms of a benign reality,
Losing the will to be separate and terrified,
How would I feel without this thought of being?
Would I stop and fall like a battery-dead toy?
Or would I shine with an eternal brightness?
A portion of the collective,
A dancing, aimless, magnificent, unknowing child.

The title of this poem comes from Byron Katie's book of the same name. I have been inspired by Byron Katie's writings and I have practised her technique, 'The Work', both on myself and with my coaching clients. This poem plays with some of Byron Katie's thoughts on the nature of reality and also combines this with similar thoughts from leading physicists. For example, in David Bohm's book 'Wholeness and the Implicate Order', he alludes to the same possibilities, although expressing these via a logical, mathematical language, in contrast with the more poetic musings of Byron Katie. Whilst I do not pretend to understand or live by all that these authors describe, I do believe that they have glimpsed something exciting and transformative. I believe that they are pioneers and that, one day, their way of looking at the world will become mainstream, and that this will lead to many positive changes in all aspects of human life. Not if, but when?

Partnerships

YOUR TURN TO SCORE the goal,
Not for competition or petty ties,
But rather to humble me with your skill,
Your turn to score the goal,
Not as a test or a silly game,
Not for anything more,
Than to keep me an equal in your eyes,
For I will not provide the help that creates dependency,
I will not create a pedestal to deny you who you are,
I will not be a 'great leader' who diminishes the common spirit we share,
Your turn to score the goal.

My turn to pass the ball,
Not for lack of guts or selflessness,
But rather to play a different role,
My turn to pass the ball,
Not as a test or a silly game,
Not for anything more,
Than to keep you as an equal in my eyes,
For I love to watch you score your goals,
I love to see you being who you are,
Creating a pedestal from which you will shout,
"My turn to the pass the ball!"

Like 'The Hinterland', this is a poem about relationships. It is only through relationships that we can experience who we are. 'The Hinterland' spoke of the risk of dominating, or being dominated, in our relationships. 'Partnerships' describes an alternative mode - a mode where the relationship has gone beyond dependency and independence to inter-dependence. It is no coincidence that the company Bill Barry and I co-founded in 2004 was called '121partners', for it was relationships of partnership that we aspired to create with each other, with our clients and with our colleagues. Partnerships are the essence of the flat organisation, which is much spoken about as a structure, but, in my experience, is not as clearly understood as a set of behaviours. The poem uses the metaphor of a sports team to describe a partnership relationship. The goal-scorer is interchangeable and refuses to be the only person scoring the goals even though that person could monopolise that role if he/she wanted to. As in sport so in leadership, where the 'great leader' can monopolise that leadership role, denying themselves and others the opportunity to work in a genuine partnership of shared responsibility. As the poem alludes, the motivation for 'passing the ball' is 100% focused on refusing to buy into a belief system that puts one person above another, which creates pedestals from which people fall. As Marianne Williamson says in her wonderful book 'A Return to Love': '..and as we let our own light shine, we unconsciously give other people permission to do the same. As we're liberated from our own fear, our presence automatically liberates others.'

Beyond the Bridge

BEYOND THE BRIDGE LIES the ocean,
Majestic in its scope and depth,
Beyond the bridge lies the final step,
The creational freedom of our dreams,
And though I dance with you, with the waves,
Though I feel the salty spray on my burning lips,
I am also that which holds us, defines us,
In its all-encompassing embrace,
Though I feel the movement of my earthly limbs,
I am also humming with the joy of the absolute,
I am that I am,
The alpha, the omega and all that's in-between,

So with this choice we become the causal field,
The creator and the created,
The architects of our world,
With this choice we bless ourselves,
And let go the final threads,
And as we leap high above the waves,
With the glee of our evolution,
We mirror the steps of our predecessors,
Evolutionary strategists all,
The insect, the fish, the amphibian,
The reptile, the mammal, the human being.

Beyond the bridge lies the truth,
A new being waits to greet us,
It is you and I and them,
Beyond the bridge lies the truth,
The great homecoming of man.

A grand poem for sure. What could be grander than this vision for the human race? A vision that we will one day replace ourselves with that which will follow us, that which is to come - a beta version, a better version. And that this will happen as an inevitable, thoughtless by-product of our consciousness, rather than as part of some grandiose human plan. For that is what has always happened on the evolutionary trail. The poem is written from the perspective of being in the sea with the fish at the time when the first one of these creatures leapt out of the water and discovered a new world - the world beyond the ocean that consisted of something we later decided to call air. How strange that must have been for that first 'fish out of water', how freaky - and with only gills with which to breathe. Not a world in which that fish could yet survive, but a world that it would never forget having glimpsed. And how would it talk about that glimpse to its fellow fish in a watery way? With great difficulty I assume. Maybe through a fishy poem or two, he/she had a go. But inside that fish and inside every fish, an evolutionary vision had been created and was stirring itself. The genie was out of the bottle, the fish was out of the water and the amphibian was already more than just a dream.

The Long Goodbye

HEAVY WITH THE LONG goodbye,
The hollow smile of a parting guest,
A flare disappears into the empty sky,
And now this fragile paper mountain,
The fruit of our love, our favourite re-creation,
Floats into a hostile and blatant world,
My dream, my baby, my work of art,
I see you plundered under the trampling feet,
Let go like a poem written, lost and never read,
And though the tears tumble across the page,
Though I ache from this endless shedding skin,
I still button my coat,
Still shine my shoes,
In readiness for a bold and future step,
For this is who I am and this is who you wanted me to be,
Heavy with the long goodbye.

This poem is about letting go and loss. I wrote it when I was grieving for my mother, who died of cancer some years ago. So it is, on the one hand, about losing something in particular ('The hollow smile of a parting guest') and, on the other, about letting go of anything you care about a great deal ('My dream, my baby, my work of art'). Whilst some may find it a depressing poem, I hope others will find the purity of its sadness uplifting. Once let go, the world does what it needs to do and you do what you need to do. Your inner fragility confronts an external world of relentless happenings. But somehow you find strength to face the future. The poem ends with a resolute steadfastness, a defiant personal declaration. What you let go taught you something very important, like a mother that long ago taught you how to button your coat, how to shine your shoes. These lessons never leave you. They are eternal in you.

The Return Path

THE DUST THAT SWIRLS ahead,
The laden treasure of a worldly quest,
Gems that fall into the deserted ground,
As my limbs ache and my eyes strain,
Caves that glisten with their wares,
A world of opportunity plundered with missionary zeal,
In a storm of forgetfulness,
Have I now the strength for the return path?

When this chill night draws in,
I cower with my claims of success,
And trade with these desperate pilgrims,
And we feel the hollowness of a conditional love,
We hear the demons that clamour for our souls,
As the camp fire smoulders,
Have I the strength for the return path?

Though I came to teach, I forgot to learn,
Though I was given a map, I became a lazy guide,
Though my first steps were true, my grip grew frail,
For I granted reality to a craven world.

Yet I know that a miracle is but a choice away,
I know that a dream takes a second to complete,
I know that the door remains open, unlocked,
The return path is here, broad and intact.

And lo, as I smile and turn away,
Fearing the solitude of toil and trek,
I feel a rush and a joy and a sudden peace,

For here are you all resplendent and made-up,
Checked-out, clean-shaven and brimming with glee,
Let us set out my friends for heaven awaits our call,
As we surge and sway on this homely course,
A crowd that throngs on the returning path.

I was reminded of this poem when talking to a colleague about the work of Joseph Campbell. Joseph Campbell was a student of mythology and developed the concept of the monomyth o r 'Hero's Journey', which identifies the various stages involved in the heroic life. Campbell suggested that these steps could be observed in all cultures throughout history. He broke the heroic cycle down into 17 steps with various poetic titles, such as 'The Call to Adventure', 'The Road of Trials' and 'The Magic Flight'. Step 15 is called 'The Crossing of the Return Threshold' and, in hindsight, I realise that this poem was written from this place on the journey. A quote from the Wikipedia article 'A Hero's Journey' summarises this step as follows: 'The trick in returning is to retain the wisdom gained on the quest, to integrate that wisdom into a human life, and then maybe figure out how to share the wisdom with the rest of the world. This is usually extremely difficult.' And later, in the same article, I came across the stunning beauty of the following description of the final stage, 'Freedom to Live': "The hero is the champion of things becoming, not of things become, because he is. 'Before Abraham was, I AM.' He does not mistake apparent changelessness in time for the permanence of Being, nor is he fearful of the next moment (or of the 'other thing'), as destroying the permanent with its change. 'Nothing retains its own form; but Nature, the great re-newer, ever makes up forms from forms. Be sure that nothing perishes in the whole universe; it does but vary and renew its form.' Thus the next moment is permitted to come to pass." What more could I possibly add?

Learning to Love Failure

KEEP ENJOYING, KEEP SHARING, keep growing, through
The ups and the downs, the lefts and the rights,
The winning, the losing, the honourable draws,
Loving the failure that allows us to live,
Loving it like our nature loves us,
For this word is too fickle to be set in stone,

Too subjective to be meaningful,
Too lame to stop us walking upright and free,
We do not know nor can we judge what is success or failure,

For our eyes are clumsy and crude,
Just short of reptilian blind,
When we say,
'Look at how I am failing',
'Look at how I am succeeding',
Someone smiles and dreams a silent dream,

Shines a silent light,
But a light so bright it will burn these medals to a crumbling dust,
Transforming our fear of failure into a shower of love,
Forgiving our forgetfulness and our lack of faith,
As all this and more recedes in the presence of the unfailing truth.

When writing this poem I had just received some feedback from a conference presentation, and this feedback was not what I had wanted it to be. Part of me felt that I had failed. The poem captures that moment - the 'down', the 'losing', the 'fickle', the 'subjective', the 'judgement'. The feedback could have laid me 'lame', i.e. it could have tempted me to withdraw, recede and lick my wounds. It could have tempted me into denial, and then I would have ploughed on regardless - insensitive and cold. Or I could have just sat here with the feeling and waited for it to pass, waited for 'the someone that smiles and the light that burns'. I could have recognised that a life fully lived must include and embrace these moments in order to be a life fully lived. For without the feeling of that moment, I would not be capable of experiencing the feeling of the other moments - the 'winning', the 'success', the 'ups', more 'judgement'. From this perspective, I was left with the ability to feel, to be human, but not to be consumed by my feelings or be limited by humanity. I was left humbled by my successes and my failures as evidence of both the glory of human consciousness and its triviality in the scheme of things.

Forever Ours to Keep

THEY'RE CROWDING IN MY throat again,
The many unspoken words,
Jostling and grasping for life,
The remnants of the truth,
Amidst my happiness they open up,
Like many petals in the sun,
Different voices from the past,
Absorbed through the perfect detail of consciousness,
Stored away under lock and key,
Now ready to walk free in this world once more,
So I breathe them into this space,
And form vibrations from the emotions they contain,
I give words to the wordless, the invisible feelings within,
And as I speak, my shoulders drop,
I admit to peace in this strange place,
I complete sentences long cut short,
I walk in rooms where I never have been,
Yet I know them through my ancestors' hearts,
Held there in my panoramic gaze,
I see a journey of struggles and pain,
Yet also a silent love, a faith and a purposeful aim.

To all those who have lifted us up,
With their invisible grace and their well-intentioned mistakes,
I now acknowledge and thank and celebrate,
To all those who died selfless and confused,
Know that this day you have been deified,
For love is eternal, yet buried deep,
Love is eternal and forever ours to keep.

As you get older and stronger and wiser then you can start to get to know your past again. Things that hurt you first time round can be re-visited from a different perspective. What once overwhelmed you emotionally no longer has that same power. This poem is about such a re-visiting of the past, a re-living, a reprocessing of what has been ('I complete sentences long cut short'). And sometimes you re-visit the past and realise that is not 'your stuff' that you are feeling, but actually the 'stuff' that was passed down to you in the collective psyche of your family, your country, your race ('I walk in rooms where I never have been'). The poem mirrors many that I have written, in that it starts from a personal perspective, but evolves into a collective awareness. As this poems reaches for its ending, the collective awareness fills the space completely and assumes a celebration. For beneath the buried hurt of personal emotions and beneath the buried hurt of collective emotions is discovered a different strata; the love of the collective consciousness. 'Love is eternal, yet buried deep, Love is eternal and forever ours to keep'. This then is the surprising reward for a bout of rueful, yet determined, introspection.

F.A.T.E. - From All Thoughts Everywhere

LET US MEET THIS with a tsunami of giving,
Let us each be nameless drops in a great wave of support,
For this is a chance to define our shared humanity,
And reclaim our common lot,
Let us find within an epicentre of love,
One that registers ten on the Richter scale,
Let us summon a shift in our perceptions,
As we rise up from humbled knees,
What then would we leave in our wake?
If not a changed landscape, a better way, a different world.

I wrote this poem on the fifth anniversary of the 2004 tsunami natural disaster, which claimed over 230,000 lives in Asia, in memory of all those who were directly affected by this cataclysmic event. It was an attempt to feel for an appropriate response to such an overwhelming, yet distant, experience. The title is taken from a passage in the book 'Conversations with God', where it is suggested that acts of fate, like a tsunami, are actually a summation of many millions of individual thoughts that coalesce to generate real-world experiences. This thinking is based on the belief that we are creative beings who have the ability to move mountains through our thoughts. Sounds crazy I know, but we have all heard the phrase 'mind over matter' and this is simply an extension of this everyday phrase. It's as crazy as every truth for which our 'flat earth' egos are not yet ready to deal with. Anyway, the poem issues a call for a different manifestation of fate, a tsunami of giving, an opportunity to use the tragedy of the tsunami to come together and define who we are and who we want to be on a global scale. And in this way too, the summation of our thoughts, words and actions has a similar power to that of the tsunami wave - itself a summation of many million innocent particles of water moving in unison. Nature reminds us that this depth of collective expression does have the power to change landscapes , internally and externally, inside and out. And we did give - 6 days after the tsunami hit Asia a total of £1bn of aid had been pledged to victims of the disaster, a huge wave of money, a huge wave of humanity. A hint at the possibilities of the human spirit.

Transition Throes

FLICKERING LIKE A KNACKERED neon,
A connection is breaking down,
Now you see me, now you don't,
Who can read in the dark?
With these half messages of mine,
The two halves of my transition throe.

Flickering like an eyelid half open,
A window in me is opening up,
Now I see you, now I don't,
Who can see with eyes wide shut?
With these sleepy lids of mine,
The two halves of my transition throe.

Learning through this flickering pain,
Glimpsing a future state of permanence,
Grasping for the excitement and joy,
Whilst flirting with the still distant past,
Waiting for the tipping point of my transition throe.

This half-finished palace resembles a dusty building site,
Yet its foundations are firm, its design a noble cause,
I will finish its construction, I will deliver the vision
And over that oaken door will I hang the garland of my new beliefs.

This poem is about change, deep change. It doesn't come much deeper than trying to change your beliefs. Beliefs are the foundation of our behaviour; when they change then everything else changes - sometimes this can be disconcerting! It is most disconcerting when you are in the halfway house between one set of beliefs and another, when you are in the midst of the transition throe. The word throe means 'a severe pang or spasm of pain, as in childbirth'. It exactly fits the feeling of giving birth to new beliefs. The old world drops away and the new world starts to take shape, and in between lies the 'flickering pain'. Yet once started the job must be finished. The new palace must be built. Determination pushes you. The vision pulls you. There is no turning back. The second verse of the poem reminds me of a quote from Marcel Proust: 'The voyage of true discovery lies not in seeking new landscapes, but in seeing with new eyes.'

Methodical Recklessness

A CHANGE IN THE weather,
A change in the times,
A shifting of sands that lie underfoot,
Staring at the ceiling at 4 am,
Stamping my feet to shake off the day,
A feeling of methodical recklessness runs through my inner world,
A sense that the bridge has been breached,
The keys lifted from idle guards,
It's happening, it's happening from the inside out.

Peculiar travel suggestions dance into my opened mind,
With secret destinations and coded travails,
All that I hear yet fear to obey,
The voice of a will that is grander than mine,
Yet grows restless ever restless at our recalcitrance.

A time for the brave,
A time for the meek,
A shift in the heavens that lie overhead,
Staring at the ceiling at 4 am,
Stamping our feet at the start of the day,
A feeling of methodical recklessness runs through the outer world,
A sense that the bridge has been built,
The latch has fallen, tumbled, shattered and free,
It's happening, it's happening from the inside out.

This poem was inspired by a conversation with Kay Cannon - a friend and fellow coach in the US. Kay was listening to me and captured my mood perfectly when she said: 'it sounds like you're engaged in methodical recklessness'. I laughed, since I loved the apparent contradiction of these two words. I said to her that it was the title of a poem and the next day I wrote it. Kay also shared with me two lovely quotes from which I pinched some of the words I used in the second verse. These were 'peculiar travel suggestions are dancing lessons from God' by Kurt Vonnegut, and 'All journeys have secret destinations of which the traveller is unaware' by Martin Buber. The poem describes an uncontrollable, unsettling, inevitable journey - a natural transformation. Maybe this would be how a flower would feel as it grew and changed if it were blessed with self-consciousness? Or, even scarier, how a caterpillar would feel when it was dying to be a butterfly? Maybe this is how the world feels when it is wanting to change, when it is bored of how things are, restless, shaking the ground and stirring the heavens? What would you be doing if you were living in times of methodical recklessness?

Reclamation

CAUGHT YOU SKULKING IN the shadows,
Scurrying from town to town,
Glimpsed you sitting at the bar in some southern hotel,
Idly stirring a cold, dank coffee-cream,
You are like a faint rash, a feint accomplice,
You are the sediment of my deepest draught,
The ridiculous dream of faithless friends,
How I would squeeze the life out of you,
Should you come within reach,
But, no, you are the unseen shadow, the slippery soap, the unscratched back,
Speak to me, you, the muted minister of my self-doubt,

Speak to me.

'Time was when I didn't need you,
Time was when I had my own life,
Time was when we were friends'

'Cast out in this splendid isolation,
Cast out to peddle like a paupered soul,
Cast out to watch, observe the distance'

'When will you let me come home?
When will you bathe me, waive the sorrows I caused? When will you heal my withered hands?'

Let's meet again you and I,
Not for gain or recrimination but just for something to do,

You know sort of like young men do,
When they know not how to tune their hearts,
Let's find the ways that rebuilt the trust once lost,
Through nothingness chats that pass the time,
And prove that we no longer have the will to kill or maim,
After you, no after you, no after you, please do,
The great skulkers stumble on in an autistic embrace,
On into the possibilities of the male condition,
On into the white light that will fuse our bones once more,
Beyond the muck and blood of our unspoken separation.

This is a poem that wrote itself. There was no thought or idea in my mind when I started it, so I suppose it is a stream of consciousness from somewhere. Something or nothing can be made of it. So what do I make of it now in hindsight? I think it is about the reality of our fragmented psyches, i.e. the idea that we are composed of many sub-personalities that vie for control and dominance and don't always agree with each other. This is the central theme of the psychological model of transactional analysis, with its sub-personalities of parent, adult and child and the internal dialogue that these 'energetic states' engage in as they struggle for their identity and role within the overall 'I'. In this poem, two sub-personalities have been fighting each other, one has won the fight and banished the other, denying it a voice or a presence until now reluctantly inviting it 'back to the table'. We hear the banished fragment pleading to return and to be forgiven. As the poem nears its ending we learn that these are two masculine sub-personalities that are not necessarily that emotionally intelligent ('The great skulkers stumble on in an autistic embrace'). Still, in their own awkward way, they seek reconciliation and the psyche reclaims its completeness. You cannot 'kill off' these internal voices without destroying your authenticity - although many of us spend many years trying to do just that.

Glittering Prize

WE CARE ABOUT THE big things,
Over which we have no control,
The famine, the flood, the state of the world,
The vision of how it could be,
Whilst the little things that lie just under our feet,
Get squashed by our clod-hopping boots,
The little screams that we do not hear,
The pained expressions we no longer see,
That which we sacrifice for a stab at fame,
In our stampede for the glittering prize.

We care about the big things,
For these are worthy of our name,
The job, the car, the next pretty house,
The vision of how it could be,
Whilst the little people that lie just at our feet,
Get squashed by our clod-hopping boots,
The little screams that we do not hear,
The pained expressions we don't see,
Those who we sacrifice for a stab at fame,
In our stampede for the glittering prize.

Remember then the little things,
Brought each day unto you,
The glance, the pause, the touching hand,
The vision of how it could be,
Gather the children that lie at your feet,
Lift them to your gaze,
Hear and see what you love as your own,
Linger in the awareness of now,

Mend then the detailed stitching of our emotional lives,
Heal the leaking spirit of our daily grind,
For those who sacrifice for a moment of love,
Render the world as a glittering prize.

Named after the Simple Minds song of the same name! An ode to the little things and the little people. It is an old, old message that I know we've all heard before. Maybe if we keep saying it over and over again, it will seep into a change in our behaviour - until the next advert, the next newspaper article, the next disapproving glance. What iron will it takes to live for the little things.

The Word

TO LIVE EACH DAY like this,
So free like blossom windswept,
To not know what is work or play or rest,
But simply steps and words and smiling back,

To live each day like this,
So full of a glorious emptiness,
To let go of the possibilities,
And share food that tastes like the first time,
Tastes like the first day of spring,
Just me and a milky sun watching on,
And there is so much time and space,
So many gaps and moments of peace,
Stepping in and out of the world,
Like a flickering movie scene,
Watching then acting then watching again,

Swept up on waves of awareness,
Swept back to gulp the air,
To live each day like this,
In a never ending picture-scape,
This then all a frame of mind,
That each carries deep within,
This then all a gift we have,
That we left at the world's front door,
This then all a living secret, a raided casket,
That we now declare as TRUTH.

'In the beginning was the Word and the Word was with God, He was in the beginning with God, All things came into being through Him….And the light shines in the darkness, and the darkness did not overtake it…..And the word became flesh and tabernacled amongst us…This was He of whom I spoke…He who comes after me has been before me….He has declared Him…I am the voice of one crying in the wilderness…behold the lamb of God who takes away the sins of the world' John 1:1-1:29. TRUTH is the word. The word is the TRUTH. Who stole the word? Who stole the TRUTH? 'A living secret, a raided casket'. Who found the word? Who found the TRUTH? You did!

The Morally Brave

THUS DECAY, UNREST AND decadence,
Provides fertile ground for new seeds,
Nature's courage knows no bounds,
Brings forth from the famine,
A feast of untold delight,
Speaks to us with compelling truth,
Brings forth the meek who have waited long,
Those who hold the heart of the age,
That which has no physical might or empirical proof,
Yet commands the lion and the lamb,
As it reaches into their common soul,
Lo, the meek will be the bravest,
When the flesh finally runs weak,
For in them the spirit burns brightest,
They carry that which does not know how to die,
That which always prevails with timeless ease,
The ark, the covenant, the grail,
The blueprint of our higher consciousness.
Sow now,
You of the highest moral ground.
Claim your inheritance, free us with your courage
As the master frees the slave.

This poem was inspired by a comment on a TV show, in which a lady exclaimed: 'What we need in this country right now is morally brave leaders!' Morally brave leaders? She was commenting on 'Broken Britain' and it made me think about the state of moral leadership in our society. On the one hand, you have the discredited leadership elite (MPs, bank CEOs, Irish priests, etc.), those addicted to the power of winning. On the other, you have the feckless folk who have given up caring and have opted out of any sense of collective responsibility. Then you have those who occupy the middle ground, the average man or woman in the street, those who are not in positions of power, but have not given up caring or taking personal responsibility. The poem suggests that it is the voice of these people that we need to hear right now, and that these people are often held back by their fear of standing out in the crowd, their fear of their own power, which they so often give away to those in the other two camps. These are the meek people whom the poem suggests must have the courage to stand up and claim their power. The poem is also a statement of conviction and trust that nature always brings forth the right answer at the right time, or, in this case, the right people at the right time. It suggests that there is a spirit lying dormant in the morally brave. This spirit will know exactly when it is the right time to stand up and speak up. This is the point when that which is broken will start to heal. Are you one of the morally brave whom nature will ask to stand up and to speak up right now? Is it time for you to reclaim the power that is given away so cheaply in every day and in every hour?

Sleep, Dream, Wake, Sleep, Dream

REFLECTIONS,
Ripples in time, compressions,
Creases in the flow,
Voices,
Leaking like oil,
I am drowning in this love,
Head bobbing above the waves,

Waves of consciousness,
Which lift and fall, lift and fall,
Leaving purple stains on my mind,
Revealing cave drawings, illiterate sounds, extinct smells,
I am drowning in this love,
Beyond loneliness, beyond boredom, beyond activity,
I am swept up on the shore of this natural habitat,
A stranger, a refugee, a stowaway,
Saved from salvation,
At least for now.
At least for now.

This is a poem about consciousness. About the boundary between sleeping and dreaming and waking up. Each night we experience a shift in consciousness when we dream. Each night we 'drown' in our dreams and then we wake up. In our dreams we see things and feel things that appear real and then we wake up. Similarly, who knows what other levels of consciousness might exist and how we 'sleep/wake up' from these? The poem speculates on this theme using the boundary between air and water as the metaphor for a shift in consciousness. Can you imagine if you had never fallen asleep in your life and then it happened to you for the first time and you felt yourself 'nodding off'? Can you imagine how frightening this would be and how much faith it would require to trust that you would wake up again in the morning? And yet without sleep we could not function, could not survive. Similarly, without love we could not function, we could not survive. Yet to lose yourself in the consciousness of love is terrifying and requires great faith. Much better to fight this temptation and save ourselves from salvation, don't you think?

Redemption Song

A FROZEN STREAM OF tears,
A bitter sweet taste left behind,
We are the memories, the vague recollections,
The agonies of knee high vulnerability,
The apron strings I couldn't hold on to,
Though I tried, I tried, I tried.

A door never opened beneath the stairs,
A space left unprotected out of love my dear,
We are the memories, the vague recollections,
In the land of the giants gentle yet firm,
The apron strings I couldn't hold onto,
Though I tried, I tried, I tried.

Only Jesus intervenes to cradle the child,
Blesses the holes left flagrant and bare,
As deep in the being a threshold holds strong,
Thou shalt not pass, shalt not penetrate,
The spirit that rose up to meet the horror of life,
Saying you're saved, you're saved, you're saved.

I will prove you with the shining light,
Stun the witness with my glaring insight,
I will be the living truth to your night of nights,
Endless, endless in my declaration of rights,
And then when I find you shivering and frail,
Will I bless you with the love of His might,
His anvil, His hammer, His peace, His sword,
Brought to you gently,
Brought to you hard.

In the light of revelations about the 'goings-on' in the Catholic church, I attempted to write something from the perspective of a victim of child abuse. We have all been victims of child abuse, it is merely a question of degree, since we have all been 'abused' by those in positions of power. Abuse comes in many forms, some more permanently damaging to the child psyche than others. As children we are vulnerable and we are trusting in an undiscriminating way. This combination of qualities can result in tragic consequences. The poem also alludes to the unique role that men play in child abuse - for it is to the female that we look for protection from the aggressive male ego ('The apron strings I couldn't hold on to, though I tried, I tried, I tried'). The irony is that even in the midst of priestly abuse, it is the human spirit that rises up in defiance to protect and save the soul ('As deep in the being a threshold holds strong'). How else could anyone survive such a shocking breach of trust? It is the defiant human spirit that commits itself to the hope of a dis-abusing future. A future in which one day the abused child stands tall and strong as an adult in front of the aged, weak and frail abuser of the past. And in that moment, the abused sheds their guilt ('endless in my declaration of rights'), feels their hidden anger in all its God-given glory ('His anvil, His hammer, His peace, His sword'), yet refuses to take revenge, trusting in the redeeming power of that which provided the original protection all those many years ago ('Will I bless you with the love of His might....Brought to you gently, brought to you hard'). God bless all those abused children - may they find it in their hearts to trust again and create a new future for us all. Amen.

All

A POOL OF WATER on a God still day,
A reflection of a heavenly sky,
A perfect, empty circle divine,
A balancing act at the centre point,
A substance which neither holds nor is held,
A vessel that neither pours nor needs filling,
Now it is lost in the background plane,
For it has no name or eminence,
Now it steps forward to perform with grace,
Like a ballerina stretched with tendons of steel,
Like a hidden hand that can reach within,
Flowing and beating and sensing itself,
Deep within this recess a new form stirs,
For in this palate of reality existent,
Are the many colours, the many shades,
All those you have copied are now well-worn,
And from this panoply, this splashed-out craze,
Comes forth this shining example,
The all of you in the all of now.

I wanted to return to a theme of potential with this poem. The first lines are representations of stillness and balance. The 'perfect, empty circle divine' is a reference to the t'ai chi symbol - 'wu chi'. 'Wu chi' is pure attention, zero emptiness, corresponding to deep sleep. It is the stillness that precedes movement, the unity that precedes the separation into 'yin' and 'yang'. It is the pregnancy that precedes creation - 'deep within this recess a new form stirs'. And then this latent, hidden potential leaps forward, announces itself amongst the current, worn-out reality, this 'splashed-out craze'. Something new is born - the 'all of you in the all of now'. Presence.

Soulburst

AND SHE CAME TO me,
Shimmering in the light of a summer dream,
She came to me,
Perfect in every detail,
Basking in the peace of God,
Speaking the words of an angel,
As if it were just any other day,
As if all were normal and in hand,
And I didn't bat an eyelid,
Couldn't even recall her words,
Because it was just any other day,
All was normal and in hand,
All was held within the peace of God,
Then waking into the sounds of a new dawn,

I smiled at this glimpse of truth,
Bottled up this glory and this joy,
Taking it with me into the buzzing crowd.

The living proof of her creation,
Sweet mother of mine.

About my mother. Rest in peace. Enough said.

Barbaric Garb

THE VICIOUS FREEDOM OF an open mind,
An empty diary, a blank sheet, a sudden start,
The rope-less ascent into a spiraling void,
Agonising a glance into the depths,
A compulsion to test the limits of my recklessness,
A rebellion from the straightened jacket of a managed regime,
To think beyond the pale where all true inspiration swirls,
To play amongst the edges where a strange peace prevails,
To lose this false sense of self, the costume, the garb,
And rest within my nature inchoate.

The vicious freedom of an open heart,
An empty head, a blank mind, a sudden start,
The rope-less descent into a glistening trove,
Agonising a glance into the depths,
A calling to accept an unlimited care-full-ness,
An obedience to the gentle chorus of a holy regime,
To be beyond the pale where all true inspiration swirls,
To play amongst the edges where a well-known peace prevails,
And rest within my nature evident.

Poetry comes from a different part of the brain. The evidence of this is when you impulsively use a word in a poem, only to later look it up in the dictionary because when you wrote it you didn't know what it meant! It then turns out to be the most apt word you could possibly have thought of. The word 'inchoate' is an example of such a word in this poem. Inchoate (in-koh-it) means 'not yet completed or fully developed'. It is not a word that I thought I knew. Where do these words come from? Where do these poems come from? For me, the experience of writing poetry is evidence that we are capable of tapping into knowing beyond our reasoning minds. Some call this intuition, some call it the 'gentle chorus of a holy regime'. Whatever we call it, 'it' clearly resides 'beyond the pale, where all inspiration swirls', and 'it' involves breaking out of the 'straightened jacket of a managed regime'. It involves an open mind and an empty heart. It is both natural and abnormal, both strange and well known, both complete and incomplete. It is clearly not logical and open to analysis, yet it has a value that we too often discount from the perspective of our 'barbaric garb'. ('Garb' – 'a mode of dress , especially of a distinctive or UNIFORM kind'). Please do not analyse this poetry – it will make you blind.

The Narrow Gate

ATTACHED AS WE ARE to all that fades,
Our clothes, our looks, our machinations,
In a society where growing old is a sin,
Like drinking sour wine, eating stale bread,
It sticks in my throat this sickly medicine,
Waiting for a new skin, a new way of living,
One that is not bought by me for me in me,
Waiting for new vessels in which to place myself,
To be reborn under water within Him,
For I have spent this life many times without,
Without relationship, without boundless joy,
Without a sense of the eternal hope springs forever,
Must whisper these words with croaking voice,
Before this world holes me like a pigeon,
Must whisper of surface glimpsed arms aloft,
Yet unless my heart opens now, great bow doors,
Unless I take in the whole of creation in one gasping gulp,
Then it will drown me outside in with a blink inconsequent,
And I will be an old hero, a war story, a collapsing coin spinning utterance,
A random power play in a terminal universe,
Stark in its choice looms the narrow gate.

Wooah! What is that all about? I sort of get the first bit (lines 1-7) - a take on consumerism and the meaninglessness of a life devoted to stuff that decays (looks, food, wine). And then there is the line about 'new vessels', which echoes the new testament verse: 'Neither do men pour new wine into old vessels' - Matthew 9:17. A reference to the fact that transformative change (a rebirth) cannot be superficial. Consumerism as a way of being that does not bring happiness and that focuses upon things, rather than relationships. The hopelessness of consumerism. And then ('Must whisper these words...') a sudden self-consciousness arising from the lapse into religious language and the stereotyping that this will provoke in others. Then finally the choice - the choice between being true to oneself or keeping up appearances. The inability to be half-pregnant ('Unless I take in the whole of creation in one gasping gulp'). A life of meaning (joy, eternal hope) or meaninglessness (coin spinning, random, terminal). The last line is another new testament reference: 'Enter through the narrow gate. For wide is the gate and broad is the road that leads to destruction, and many enter through it' - Matthew 7:13. Is it any clearer now?

Letting You Down

I NEVER LET YOU down,
Never let you off my back,
Kept you there because you knew good jokes,
And whispered them in my ear,
As I laughed I was tempted to forget,
That my legs were aching so,
As I laughed I was tempted to forget,
That I carried you down my path,
A pact we made that served us well,
Through many a difficult day,
But with it crept in our dependency,
And a pinch of grief and jealousy,
A twist of judgement and complacency,
So now I let you down at last,
Onto your wasting limbs that will find their feet,
I let you down at last,
Finally giving each back the independence that we stole many years ago,
The crown jewels that are now restored,
In the castles of our forgiven hearts.

I wrote this poem many years ago following the breakdown of a valued relationship. I was reminded of it yesterday. Dependency is a theme that I am somewhat obsessed with, or you could say I am passionate about. How does dependency develop in relationships? What is each party's contribution to this? How is independence gained? And what about inter-dependence? How is this different and how can we establish this in our relationships? The poem describes a dependent relationship that has served its full course and ends. In a dependent relationship, one carries and one is carried. A deal is struck to which both parties agree, and which serves them until the day it does not. Put bluntly, the deal is: 'I'll carry you and in return you'll make me laugh' ('kept you there because you knew good jokes'). This sounds trite but is not far from the truth. One party takes responsibility for the practical affairs and the other is free from this. In their freedom they think more creatively, they travel lightly, they can live for the day (well, wouldn't you in their position?). It is important to stress that I am not blaming anyone for this or saying it is wrong, it is just an observation and an experience that I have had. However, the difficulty with dependent relationships is that they are not holistic, they tempt us to dishonour our full selves ('the crown jewels'), and this is difficult to sustain over long periods of time without getting tired - emotionally and spiritually. Often, dependent relationships end. But sometimes they don't and sometimes they evolve into inter-dependent relationships. This one didn't. In this case, it had gone too far.

Fight, Flight or Forgiveness

THESE BLOWS WE ARE feeling,
Which still feel real,
And they hurt and swell with pain,
They tempt us to run away,
Or to stand and fight and brawl,
For we think it is real,
And yet we can let it happen,
Like watching a movie scene,
We can be author not actor in this dream,
Distant and observant and still,
Whilst the blows are raining down,
And your ego is screaming for revenge,

And then the rage passes,
Like an impersonal storm that dies,
And you have not fought nor run away,

You are still standing, it was not real,
And now,
With the energy of forgiveness flowing in your limbs,
You move forward again as a leader in this world.

For me this poem is an aspiration. I see that it could be possible to take this approach in all situations, however challenging, yet I still find it difficult to put it into practice. I find that I do not run away and I do not fight, but I do get hurt by just standing still. The reason I get hurt is because my powers of forgiveness are not strong enough to create a sufficiently strong 'impersonal field'. There comes a point at which I do take things personally, even if my outward behaviour does not betray this fact. On the one hand, these situations show me the edge of my development, but I also wonder about protection. There are some situations in which it is sensible and prudent not to be defensive or aggressive, but to have appropriate protection. Not to have protection might be naïve, and it might over-estimate your strength. We know that in a physical conflict, protection might take the form of a shield. What is the equivalent of a shield in a situation where it is not a physical attack, but an emotional or spiritual attack? I don't know the answer to this question, but I am sure going to work on it because there are plenty of pointy-shaped things out there. Beyond the purely personal context of this poem, I do chime with its last line where forgiveness is positioned as a critical leadership competence for the complexities of the modern world. In how many corporate HR manuals does this word appear?

A Labour of Love

IT'S A GAME, A factory, a vainglorious point-scoring institution,
Chews you up, spits you out, drags your entrails in the streets for all to sneer,
When you stand in front of those Victorian spires, those iron gates,
When you enrol and enrol and enrol again,
And hear them screaming for your soul,
The good, the great and the simply profane,
Clambering over your inert frame,
Wanting you for their GDP, their endless needs, their sycophantic, meaningless parade,
Makes your heart hammer your insides raw,
Like a battered iron casing,
Your intuition holds fast in the teenage storm,
Compels you, drives you, on and on,
Away from that which wishes to feed on you,
That which you never understood,
Except in your aching guts,
Except in the love of your Mother's arms.

And years later you come to rest,
Washed up, burnt out, heaving up,
Dizzy with relief that they didn't devour you with their snarling teeth,
All those loyal soldiers didn't catch you with their relentless, pounding drums,
Your gift is intact, shining like a lost pearl,
Glistening like an eternal promise, a sacred shrine,
Deep in the unplundered depths lies this protected, defenceless truth,

That which they wanted to steal from you with their grasping claws,
With their greedy, zealous, engineering minds,
That which was only ever yours to keep.
And now, as the shawl draws back,
It looks up at you like a little baby and smiles a little baby's smile,
It blinks in wonder at the sheer magnificence of it all,
Crawls into the light with its blinking eyes,
Pulls itself up tall just by your side,
Summons the strength of 2,000 pointless years,
And strides purposefully into this starving world.

This poem is older than most in this collection. I would guess that it was written at some time in the nineties. It is a cynical reflection on my experience of the education system – a system which has served me well in many respects. I have collected an impressive array of certificates from various academic institutions, which I am proud of. For sure, the education system has developed my thinking brain, yet has it developed my heart and my spirit to the same degree? I think not. It was John Wesley who said 'An ounce of love is worth a pound of knowledge', yet our education system does not mirror this principle in my experience. In contrast, to preserve and protect your heart and your spirit in this fiercely competitive and individualistic culture is a lonely and desperate struggle against the odds. I thank God that He has protected my own soul, despite the endless temptations to 'sell out' to the many who wished to use the talents He gave me for their own selfish ends.

A Stumbling Grace

BEEN SWEPT UP BY the storms of life,
Been swept down by the retreats,
Lost my balance in your absence,
Lost my rock, lost my way,
Made a rash move with a tearful eye,
Stood tall though my legs were thin,
And now it comes to this, a stumbling grace,
To this a stumbling grace it comes.

I give thanks for all I've been given,
I try not to question what's taken away,
I remember all the words and moments,
And know what I was blessed to share,
But still it stings like a salted wound,
Still it catches me in the throat,
And now it comes to this a stumbling grace,
To this a stumbling grace it comes.

Pray calm me with your presence Lord,
Send your host to steady the ship,
Drown me with your choir of angels,
For I sense I will lose my grip,
Long is the day and longer the night,
Yet I resign myself to your might,
And so it comes to this a stumbling grace,
To this a stumbling grace it comes.

This poem is about letting go and loss. I watched a TV programme recently, in which George Michael(!) said: 'The world is split into two very different groups of people - those who have experienced a great loss in their lives and those who have not yet reached that point'. I think this is fair. Great loss does change your perspective in a fundamental way. I think this is because great loss shakes your identity to its roots and challenges your sense of security at a profoundly deep level. The best that you feel you can do is to stumble on, yet to do so with grace and not with anger or with guilt. The stumbling is appropriately human because to not stumble when you experience loss is to be heartless, inauthentic and absurdly strong. The grace is appropriately divine because it is who you are in the midst of your loss that defines your example and your impact on others, as well as your relationship with the higher power who you perceive to have taken away what you valued so highly. The third verse of this poem is the moment of surrender - the tipping point when fighting the pain of loss finally gives way to the truth of our vulnerability and our despair. The point at which we finally, finally ask for help and submit ourselves to a new covenant with that which has a higher power over our lives. For individuals this is a process of weeks, months and years. For entire societies this is a process of months, years and decades. For all we know, for a whole race it could easily take at least 2,000 years.

Ha Ha English

Why can't the English speak the truth?
Are we so civil, are we so anglicised?
In our stripy pyjamas, in our public houses,
What secrets do these tight lips hide?
A nation with too much history, too many heroes,
Too many carpets bulging with that swept under,
So now we don't speak in case we belch rudely,
We don't play cricket because it never stops raining,
We don't go through the door if we can go round the houses,
And we laugh, laugh so hard, at the irony of it all.

Why can't the English tie their own boot laces?
Are we so privileged, are we so busy shouting?
In our guilty moments, in our filthy milky way,
What did Victoria do to Albert in that museum?
A nation with too much front and much left behind,
Too many Romany Rooney ruby-faced lotharios,
So now we don't speak in case we belch loudly,
We don't play cricket because we never stop swearing,
We don't go through the door we go round the back passage
And we laugh, laugh so hard, at the irony of it all.

Laughing, laughing so hard,
All the way to the bank,
And back again,
Distraught, disgraced,
So hard,
Laughing,
At us,
Can't you see they're

Laughing,
All the way,
To where the bank used to be,
Laughing,
So hard,
Aren't we?

    This is a flippant poem with a saucy sense of humour. The sort of humour you get on postcards at English seaside resorts. It feels like it must have been written near closing time in the local pub, because of its mixture of hilarity and a sense of impending reckoning. It captures a hysterical sadness and hints at serious problems below the surface, unspoken, swept under carpets and contained by the English habit of irony, politeness and understatement. Even Wayne Rooney makes a surprise appearance as an icon of the times - distraught, disgraced. And our banks - distraught, disgraced. Ourselves - distraught, disgraced, but still laughing. Aren't we?

Friend or Foe

MY MIND UNRAVELS LIKE frayed cotton,
It jumps, it stumbles, it starts, it stops,
An unreliable witness and a faltering friend,
It gnaws at the bone of my identity,
As if it's activity were the key and the touchstone,
My, it is so high and mighty,
Yet perched on the cliff edge of its own arrogance,
My, it is so convinced and convincing,
Spinning out half lies and half-truths half-heartedly,
We fall together wrapped in stale question marks,
Fall together forever poking at our pointless wit,
The 'I' and the 'me' and the grasping for the future,
Like Job and all his learned, impassioned friends,
Casting out pronunciations on this, that, the other,
Like we know, like we could even touch the hem,
Of the intricate blazing glory that doth surround us,
The crushing detail of each second's magnificence,
The sea of heaven's complexity in which we swim,
Yet we dare not drown, dare we?
We who are lost, so lost, in the supremacy of human ideology.

This is a poem about the human mind. It asks the question as to whether our mind is our friend or our foe. It challenges our habit of forming opinions based on limited data, and yet holding to these opinions as facts. It reminds me of the work of Professor Chris Argyris on what he calls the 'ladder of inference'. Argyris states: 'We live in a world of self-generating beliefs which remain largely untested. We adopt those beliefs because they are based on conclusions, which are inferred from what we observe, plus our past experience. Our ability to achieve the results we truly desire is eroded by our feelings that i) Our beliefs are the truth ii) The truth is obvious iii) Our beliefs are based on real data iv) The data we select are the real data.' Why does this human habit get in the way of us achieving what we truly desire? I think the clue to the answer to this question lies in the last five lines of the poem ('Like we know...') - our mind needs to create boundaries and limits in order to give itself a separated identity. It has to do this in order to form any opinion at all because it needs, at an absolute minimum, a subject and an object. It needs an 'I'. Yet the moment it seeks this identity, it loses its sense of awe and its sense of unlimited possibilities. As we set our many goals and resolutions let us be aware of this tricky character - the monkey mind!

The Gold

BEHIND THE GUILT I found the anger,
Behind the anger I found the gold,
The gold of courage,
The gold of peace,
The gold for which I had long dug deep,
The gold that glistened,
The gold that stung,
A thousand memories,

A thousand truths,
Behind the guilt I found the anger,
Behind the anger I found the gold,
The gold of courage,
The gold of peace,
The gold of redemption,

Forever ours to keep.

Feelings are tricky characters, aren't they? Forever hiding under layers of intellectual thought and scurrying away when you try to track them down. You grab them by the tail and they twist and squirm trying to avoid being pulled into the light of day, preferring to skulk in the darker recesses of your being and pounce at their own choosing and in their own disruptive way. This simple poem describes trying to chase the emotion of guilt, focusing on it very hard, until it passed away and was replaced by a deeper and more fundamental feeling of anger. When this was in turn focused on and allowed to express itself, then it too passed away and behind that - the gold! A positive feeling suddenly emerged - a feeling of courage and peace. These deeper feelings are often older in their origin, yet can only be felt when other, more recent, feelings have been given their due notice. They can also be more powerful, like a classic vintage that has been kept for a special day. Yes, funny old things these feelings.

Against the Grain

CARRYING TORCHES WITH PURPLE flames,
In a circle of white robes,
My hand steady on yours,
Fear not the hidden world of shadows,
Where nothing is quite as it seems,
Though you are wide awake yet you sleep,
Amongst the radiance of life's creating forces,
And one click of my fingers is all it needs,
One dipping of the bread and casual aside,
For these powers to rupture reality's sheen,
Your faith will heal you, your love remains,
All else slips through our hands like sand,
On the shores of an infinite impossible sea,
Gold and blue and red with cherubs and more,
We bask in the profound mysteries of our forefathers,
And glory that a grain of knowledge itches so.

One night, I was talking to my wife, Jane about the unconscious mind. Not your average 'over the dinner table' conversation, but it did seem to grab our interest for a while. We got onto the phrase 'poetic license' and whether this means being given permission to talk nonsense under the guise of being artistic. Naturally, I felt compelled to share one of my poems with Jane at this point so I read her 'Against the Grain'. At the end of a dramatic and fluent recital, I looked up and Jane said 'That's nonsense!', to which I replied 'No, it's poetic license'. She said 'Well, what does it mean?' and I said 'It's a poem about the unconscious mind and the hidden, yet powerful, role it plays in our lives. 'Fear not the hidden world of shadows, Where nothing is quite as it seems'. Because even when we think we are operating from our conscious mind the unconscious is still at work. 'Though you are wide awake yet you sleep, Amongst the radiance of life's creating forces'. Under hypnosis or in the presence of a great spiritual teacher then a simple physical gesture can trigger a trance. 'And one click of my fingers is all it needs, One dipping of the bread and casual aside, For these powers to rupture reality's sheen'. We suddenly question what it is real and who is really in charge. 'Your faith will heal you, your love remains, All else slips through our hands like sand'. And we are dazzled by the amazing possibilities of this colourful new world. 'On the shores of an infinite impossible sea, Gold and blue and red with cherubs and more, We bask in the profound mysteries of our forefathers'. This glimpse of something different, something endless and beyond our grasp. 'And glory that a grain of knowledge itches so'. Does that make sense to you?

Freedom to Live

WINGSPAN UNKNOWN THIS GOLDEN bird,
Colonies diverse in stale undergrowth,
Leaves that sway, reeds that bend,
Sound of the deepest, bluest seas,
Gait of the man with nothing to lose,
Ripple of the water in a cup of tea,
View from the bridge, the mountain, the pier,
Taste from the spice, the sauce, the lube,
Touch of an angel, still by my side,
Glimpse of a future, certain and free,
Blessing of a son who is taller than me,
Beating of a heart deep inside of thee,
Fingers in the pie, pennies in the stream,
This the rising chorus of a sensual parade,
This the flooded plain of my consciousness,
The glory, the beauty, the sheen of pain,
This the puzzle, the picture, the place in between,
The sense, the nonsense, the proliferate world,
The panoply, the Pandora, the gaping box,
Bulging, splitting, stretching from its full countenance,
Timeless, endless, wordless peace,
The freedom to live,
And the freedom to die,
Asleep in your arms,
Asleep in your arms,
The freedom to live,
And the freedom to die,
Asleep in your alms,
Asleep in your alms.

This poem is an indulgent play on words. It is a rush of phrases that initially appear to have no real connection. Yet it is immensely sensual - sights, sounds, tastes, touches. It is uplifting in its scale and range. The reader feels as if they are being taken on some grand tour of natural reality - a thrilling perspective, a sensual parade. With this airborne lightness comes a bursting, exhilarating freedom - the freedom to live. As in many of my poems, the unconscious is seizing its moment to take over the controls and flood the mind with its unique, mysterious, eternal vision. It quickly sidesteps words and substitutes a level of real experience that is excruciating in its intensity. Finally, the conscious mind is overwhelmed and falls asleep. A deep sleep. Asleep in your arms - who's arms? Asleep in your alms. Alms? In Buddhism, alms or alms-giving is the respect given by a lay Buddhist to a monk or nun. It is not charity as presumed by Western interpreters. It is closer to a symbolic connection to the spiritual and to show humbleness and respect in the presence of normal society. The act of alms-giving assists in connecting the human to the monk or nun and what he or she represents. Bless you.

Cloying Vines

CLOYING VINES OF guilt,
Trip you up,
Hold you down,
Keep you small,
Tempt you into responsibility,
Tempt you into carrying other people's burdens,
Whilst they sleep light and flutter free,
Cloying vines of guilt,
Bred from a crime you did not commit,
The crime of the hungry wolves,
Who devoured your innocent soul,
So you could cover their tracks,
And dress them up, worship them, serve them,
Free them from their tears through your fear,
Of living in a godless loveless world,
Cloying vines of guilt,
A jungle of rampant undergrowth,
Yet one in which you have built a lonely home,
A sense of shrouded security,
A prison for your dreams and divinity,
Until the scales fall from your eyes,
And the catastrophic truth sets you free,
I did not crucify God's son,
Neither did you,
The redeemer redeemed,
And the ascension prevailed.

I wrote this poem following a conversation I had with an old friend. We were discussing our needs and how we felt when we stood up for our needs. This felt difficult for both of us, because we felt guilty about appearing needy and we feared the reaction and judgement of others. Somehow, somewhere we learnt that to express our inner needs and expect these to be met was not our right. No, this was the right of others and it was our duty, our loyal duty, to meet the needs of others. This is what we were taught as the natural order of things, except it is not natural at all. Yet, if this is how we define love and care in a mutual relationship, then this is what we will get. If this is all you have known, then how can you imagine more without triggering the 'cloying vines of guilt'. This is a truly devious lie and one which it takes great courage to unravel and to face. For who's guilt is it that you are choosing to carry if it is not your own? Who originally outsourced this guilt to you and tempted you into accepting it, if not someone who you thought you could trust? Hence, as you follow this trail you arrive at the 'catastrophic truth' - there have been 'hungry wolves' in your life and you did not recognise them and you still do not recognise them, for to do so leaves you without your dream. Hence you wander along, naive and hoping it won't happen again; attracting those very wolves and their ravenous desires. The last four lines of the poem contain the keys to unlock this prison. I have expressed them in religious terms, yet this is only one way of phrasing things. In essence, these words are the instant release from guilt.

The Dogs are Coming

NOTHING IS SUBVERSIVE, NOTHING is sacred,
All the lines are blurred, the scenery shifting,
You don't know where you stand,
Because what you stand on is sinking,
What you are breathing is a mixture,
Of this and that, that and his,
You are hypnotised, yes, you are hypnotised,
Entranced, in trance and goggle-eyed,
Your conscious mind is asleep,
So in flies the buzzing host of lies,
Your doors are swinging open unhinged,
It scares the horses this whispering wind,
That you let in, let in, keep letting in,
You are hypnotised, yes, you are hypnotised,
Unprotected defiled by a daily diatribe,
Bent double by undigested flak and flak,
Pummeled flat by a stampeding herd,
Who heard that you were easy fare,
Rope-less, hopeless, loves shattered pride,
Left in the gutter with nothing to hide,
Are you now satisfied that,
Unlike this poem,
Your dream,
Will never,
End?

Sometimes poems just come and there is no stopping them. It's like having a bad case of the runs. This was certainly true for this poem. I was on the 9.20 train to London, just pulling into Euston and musing about Beyonce appearing at The Glastonbury festival in 2011. 'Nothing is subversive any more' I thought, 'not even Glastonbury', and then I heard someone else in my head say 'Nothing is sacred either'. Then I heard 'All the lines are blurred' and I hurriedly got out my iphone and started writing. The problem was that the train had come to a halt and I needed to get off, but I couldn't stop, so I was walking down the platform still tapping on my phone - 'What you are breathing is a mixture'. Then I was on the underground trying to stay on my feet as the carriages swayed - 'defiled by a daily diatribe'. Next, I was waiting for my client in their office reception - 'Left in the gutter with nothing to hide'. All the time I am thinking why can't you wait? Why can't you wait? Well, I got my answer because after my coaching session I met a friend and found myself reading this freshly born poem to them. I finished reading it and suddenly declared: 'Maybe this poem is for you, but it has no title?' 'The Dogs are Coming' my friend replied, as if stating the blindingly obvious 'The title is 'The Dogs are Coming'. 'Yes' I replied 'The Dogs are Coming - that is the title'. So that is it. That is how poems are made. A very personal poem for a very specific person. As such it is private and I am not going to explain it any more to you, so there!

Lamentation

ENGLAND'S GREAT HEART BLEEDS tonight,
Heavy tears roll down her cheeks,
Her eyes burn like a sad destitute,
She lives in a ransacked home,
Her windows are smashed, her pockets picked,
Her back yard a blazing din,
Her children run wild like dogs unleashed,
Her neighbours keep peering in,
The fragile veneer of a civilised life,
Punctured, pierced pulled apart at the seams,
Like a one-armed rag doll left to rot,
In a puddle of stale, petulant dreams,
Where once was a cause worth fighting for,
Now consumes a paradise emptiness,
Where once was the cross a raliying call,
Now in exile unpleasant land caught,
Green only with envy for the cele-bratty plight,
A mere shadow of her former life.

(Lament, lament, lament,
Children of the golden calf,
Smashed tablets, PCs, correct politicale,
Repent, repent, repent,
Children of the grafted vine,
For the authority you so disdain,
Is soon to attest its might.)

Some words dedicated to the 1 4 - year- old looters who sprang up in towns across the country like wild mushrooms overnight during the riots of 2011. The first lines remind us that this is our country, we all make it what it is and what shames one shames us all. This is my house, your house, our back yard, our children running amok whether you like it or not. The poem migrates into a skit on the hymn Jerusalem with its 'green and pleasant land' and points at an idolatry that has taken root in the soul of the country - the worship of a consumer-paradise emptiness. The bracketed lines refer to passages from the bible, specifically Exodus 32:1-35 and Romans 11:17-24. You don't have to read these if you don't care. The tablets referred to could be tablet PCs or the sacred tablets of Moses - who knows, who cares? The authority referred to could be that of the police or that of God - who knows, who cares? Do you?

Facing it Down

THIS ENEMY I AM fighting,
Believes it has its teeth in me,
With its final desperate strike,
Believes it can haunt my soul,
With its premonition of darkness,
It taunts with mocking grin,
'Just who is the ruler here?',
It fears that I am about to spill and speak,
About to escape from this dirty prison,
And it is right come win, lose or draw,
It is right that this is the showdown,
Let us face it now why not?
For one of us must be right, the other wrong,
Let us have it out now, why not?
For my only sickness is doubt,
My only weakness is clinging on,
To the vain idea of my body's reality,
I will not cower in the presence of evil,
I will not shrink back from the truth,
If I fall I wish to fall on a warrior's battlefield,
Charging towards love with a scent of steel,
If I fall I wish to fall laughing at my little self,
Declaring an example that inspires my kin,
Blesses their future path with a showering gold,
So I pull out the fiery darts that pierced my chest,
Spit on the ground that still withstands my frame,
Summon the hordes who have waited this day,
Since paradise was lost and infernos burned,
Let us take this citadel of our lifetime's fear,
Ransack and plunder the demons within,

In the name of all who tonight shake and weep,
Let us cry 'Release! Release!' in unified roar,
Let us burn every shred of the imposter's lair,
Grimacing at the ruthlessness of virtue's claim,
And waking with a pledge never to relinquish again.

I wrote this poem in a period when I was experiencing panic attacks about my health. I was driving to a hotel near Oxford and I started getting stinging pains in my chest. I had felt these pains over a couple of weeks and it was frightening me. I had started to create dark images in my mind; images of heart attacks and ambulances and the like. As I drove, I played out these vivid fantasies in my mind and I got more and more scared. When I got to my destination I gave myself a good talking to and said 'Right, I am making a stand on this here and now! Let's face this down.' So I went to the bar, bought a pint and wrote these words. It was like breaking an evil spell that had got a hold of me and it was time to show it who was the boss of my mind, the boss of my thoughts - ME! Ultimately, I worked myself into an equal and opposite frenzy of courage and defiance amidst a glorious honourable death. In effect, I was creating a new movie in my mind and, through this poem, making it vivid, inspiring and real. As is often the case in my poetry, the words move from the personal to the collective as I broaden out the message from my own puny panic attack to all the worried and the doubting and the frightened people in the world. It gives me strength to do this and I hope it gives you strength too. Of course, a few days later I went to visit the doctor and was diagnosed with the not-often-fatal condition of 'acid reflux'! And I am okay with you having a good laugh at my expense at this point, so long as you can put your hand on your own heart and tell me you have never, ever had any crazy little fears that have remotely ruled your life.

Letting Go

EVERY DAY YOU'RE dying,
Yet some days I feel fine,
Every day I'm dying,
Yet some days you feel fine,
Every day there's weather,
Yet some days the wind blows hard,
Every day I think these thoughts,
Yet some days I let them go,
Like so many colours,
Like so many shades,
All the tones,
All the gradients,
All the textures,
All the fragrances,
All the moments,
All the spaces,
All the fragments we have,
Yet some days I let them go.

In the play of the relative,
Do we find our experience of life,
That which we love and crave,
In the play of the relative,
Do we define a concept called 'I',
Yet, one day will 'I' let go.

Increasingly, as I study hypnotic communication, I realise that poems are essentially hypnotic scripts. Poems use a lot of the techniques of hypnotic communication to confuse the conscious mind and therefore to open up a channel of communication with the unconscious mind or minds -the many 'mini-minds', as they are referred to in Havens & Walters' fascinating book 'Hypnotherapy Scripts'. This simple poem contains some good examples of these techniques. First, it uses a repetitive number of what are known in hypnosis as 'universal quantifiers' - words such as 'every', 'some', 'all'. Universal quantifiers are vague and non-specific, hence they prompt the reader to seek their own interpretation of the words from their own deeper meaning - it is the unconscious mind that provides this meaning by throwing up a picture, a sound or a feeling in the reader's conscious mind. The poem also contains what linguists refer to as a 'lack of referential index'. In plain English, what this means is that in the phrase 'Every day you're dying', it is not clear who the 'you' is. Is it referring to the reader? Is it referring to a friend or relative of the poet? Again, it is not clear, hence the reader is prompted to provide their own meaning and the unconscious mind will provide that, won't it? ('tag question') Then there are things known as 'nominalisations', an example of which is the noun 'weather'. Weather does not exist in the real world, it is a made-up concept. And then there are metaphors - in this poem the weather is used as a metaphor, the changing weather that never stays the same and is therefore continually letting go. It would all be very clever if these words were written by the conscious mind, but of course they were not and that is what ultimately makes for the difference between machines and man. Now let go.

From Sense to Nonsense

I LISTEN WITH MY conscious mind,
I explore with searching questions,
To help you recover your deeper truth,
Which is your truth not mine, that's right,
I validate your world with all my being,
Seeing you,
Hearing you,
Feeling you move,
And then when it is my turn to speak,
I switch off my conscious mind,
For all it wishes to do is tell you how clever it is,
I turn on my unconscious, all-knowing mind,
With poetry, imagination, vague artistry and sleight,
I speak to that part of you which also knows and believes,

English for the English,
French for the French,
Different languages for different people in different lands.

Dancing pairs that glide and exchange and flow,
Balancing on one leg with arms outstretched,
A physical crossing and re-crossing of arms and square pegs,

In square holes, round pegs in round holes,
That's right and this is all that is left behind,
For how else could you walk or recognise my face.

I had fun writing this! It is just playing around with the concepts of the conscious and unconscious minds, which is my current fascination in coaching. When I coach, I increasingly try to listen with my conscious mind and speak with my unconscious mind, and this poem tries to explain why. The conscious mind is great at paying attention to things, focusing on the words, the sights and the personal impact of the individual. The conscious mind can also design searching questions that prompt the listener to recover the more detailed and specific experience of their personal reality. As you listen so intently, it is then easy to drop into a trance. As the individual drives deeper into their internal experience it is easy to drop into a trance - that's right. Then when speaking, do not disturb the trance with the vain posturing of the conscious mind. Switch it off and speak from that place where we all write poetry - the unconscious mind. French for the French. English for the English. Then you can find the balancing point of conscious listening and unconscious speaking to trigger the awesome resources of the individual's unconscious mind - the resources that taught them how to walk without a user manual and enables them to recognise up to 10,000 faces at any point in time.

Dissociation

COLLAPSING INTO PEACE AND relaxation,
Brick by brick the old house falls,
They say it was brave to destroy this lair,
But it felt inevitable in every way,
For is it brave when a rusty leaf falls to the ground?
Is it brave when the caterpillar cocoons itself in darkness?
Or is it just nature following its ceaseless course?
Necessary endings are the norm you see, you hear,
For in this way is the soil tilled for seeds of future growth,
In this way our hearts are scoured of the crust of pride,
That which tempts us into a false magnificence,
Today our grip on the wheel is loosened at last,
So collapsing into peace and relaxation,
We admire the view from the Director's chair.

This poem was written in a time of personal change - a time when it felt like things were collapsing around me. Others felt I was being brave in choosing change, but that is not how it felt to me. It was just a natural process governed by the heart. Also, I was being humbled (again!), having got used to the status and the status quo of an easier life. To build something new can often involve demolishing something old along the way - that doesn't always feel great at the time. But if we had the faith of a caterpillar, the faith of a leaf, then we would trust the ultimate outcome of a process of transformation. Endings are part of the cycle. The 'letting go' theme runs through this poem strongly, as it does with others I have written. I love the idea of being able to take up a perspective from the 'Director's chair'. As well as the religious connotation, this image reminds me of the NLP technique of dissociation and hence gave the poem its title. If you dissociate from an experience then you step outside of it and observe it from a distance. This is a good technique for reducing the emotional impact of bad memories. In contrast, it is great to associate with good memories - step inside them and look at the scene through your own eyes. Caterpillars must be great at disassociation as they sit in that cocoon wondering what the hell is going on, don't you think?

The Watchmen and the Wolves

YEH, I SENT WATCHMEN to guard the walls,
To watch for wolves amidst the sheep,
To watch for the enemy riding on the dawn,
Yet when watchmen fall weary the holes appear,
Holes in our hearts, holes in our souls,
Holes in the fabric that hold the centre in place,
Holes in your families, your leaders, your protectors all,
When the watchmen fall weary the stains appear,
Stains on your floors, stains on your uniforms,
Stains on the reputations of those I sent to keep you,
Stains in your dreams, your words, your conscience all,
And the wolves are amongst you, ravaging and wild,
Where were my watchmen?
Where was the anger that seals my sacred chamber?
Where were the locks, the barricades on my holy house?
For all are guilty for the good they did not do,
Where were my watchmen?
Where were my watchmen?
When the wolves kept on coming, kept on coming,
And where is the one who has the faith?
The faith to see the totality of darkness on the land,
Yet still believe in the light that the darkness hides,
Where is the one who has the courage?
The courage to see the totality of darkness on the land,
Yet rise up with the anger of a thousand guilty memories,
Declaring the axiom of the new age,
'Yeh tho thy passed this way, thy pass this way no more'
'Yeh tho thy picked my pockets, thy pick them no more'
'Yeh tho thy corrupted me with thy serpent eyes, thy are now blind'

'Yeh tho I slept on His duty, I now stir with His strength'
'Yeh, tho I was lost, now am I found in His love'
'Yeh tho the darkness reigned, it did not capture my heart',
And in the distance I spy the wolves gathering once more,
Approaching the walls of Jerusalem in droves,
Not knowing that today we fulfil the dreams of Isaiah,
Today we strike down the wolves at our doors,
With authority and with justice and with the might of the meek.
Today we lift the veil, today we claim the truth.

This poem was inspired by a coaching session I was holding, in which the coach suddenly exclaimed: 'This reminds me of that passage from Isaiah!'. To which I replied with some astonishment 'Which passage?' "You know, Isaiah 62:6 - 'I have posted watchmen on your walls O Jerusalem, they will never be silent day or night." After the session, I read the passage again and also read Isaiah 56:10: 'Israel's watchmen are blind, they all lack knowledge; they are all mute dogs, they cannot bark, they lie around and dream they love to sleep. They are dogs with mighty appetites; they never have enough'. Next I was writing, and I was reminded of the rising tide of accountability in the world right now - MPs expenses, the banking crisis, the Arab spring. It is as if we have collectively let things happen on our watch, stuff that has crept up on us in our societies and suddenly we are waking up from a collective trance, looking around and saying 'What on earth happened round here?' Holes have appeared. Stains have appeared. Locks have been picked. Yet suddenly we see it so clearly and we know it is not acceptable any more. There is anger in people's hearts, a witch-hunt afoot, a wolf-hunt. Yet be careful for the trail may lead to your own door. For as we call out the wolves amongst us, let us not forget that we were the watchmen who slept, who did not bark, who couldn't get enough when we could get it and who failed to protect that which needed our protection.

About the Author

Through his work in the business world as an entrepreneur, corporate leader and executive coach, John has witnessed the potential of personal coaching and mentoring to unlock the faith, vision and inspiration of senior business leaders. He discovered his own faith 15 years ago at the age of 34 as a result of receiving intense coaching in the workplace. More recently, through writing books and speaking at leadership conferences, he has recognised his own calling to share the good news of a personal Christian faith with a secular leadership audience.

John is married to Jane and they live in Solihull, United Kingdom, with their two sons, Robert and Patrick. He is a member of Solihull Christian Fellowship. Outside of poetry and his Christian faith, his work is influenced by his passion for systems thinking, his expertise in t'ai chi and his extensive experience working with Olympic athletes and their coaches.

For more details on his experience in the workplace, please visit http://www.linkedin.com/in/johnblakey and for more details of his book 'Challenging Coaching', co-authored with Ian Day, please visit www.challengingcoaching.co.uk. John can be contacted via john@johnblakey.co.uk.

If you have enjoyed reading this book, please take the time to write a review of it on Amazon UK so that others may gauge its relevance to their own needs and interests. Thank you.

Printed in Great Britain
by Amazon.co.uk, Ltd.,
Marston Gate.